PIANO • VOCAL • GUITAR

COLE PORTER
22 CLEVER AND FUNNY SONGS

ISBN 0-7935-2632-9

HAL•LEONARD®
CORPORATION

7777 W. BLUEMOUND RD. P.O. BOX 13819 MILWAUKEE, WI 53213

D1595553

COLE ALBERT PORTER

JUST THE FACTS...

BORN: Peru, Indiana June 9, 1891

MOTHER: Kate Cole

FATHER: Samuel Fenwick Porter

FAMILY BUSINESS: farming, timber and coal

SIZE OF THE PORTER LAND HOLDINGS: 750 acres

ESTIMATED AMOUNT OF COLE'S INHERITANCE FROM HIS FAMILY: $1,000,000 - $1,500,000

EDUCATION: Worcester (Massachusetts) Academy, 1905-1909, at Yale University, 1909-1913, Harvard University Law School, 1913-14, and again at Harvard University (Music), 1915-1916

COLLEGE SONGS BY CP: "Bingo Eli Yale" and "Bull Dog"

MILITARY SERVICE: French Foreign Legion, 1917-1919

MARRIED: to heiress Linda Lee Thomas, December 1919, Paris

FIRST PUBLISHED SONG: "The Bob-O-Link Waltz" 1902 (vanity publication)

COMPOSITION TEACHER IN PARIS: Vincent d'Indy, for composition, counterpoint, harmony and orchestration

FIRST SONG ON BROADWAY: "Esmerelda" in *Hands Up*, opened July 22, 1915

FIRST COMPLETE SCORE ON BROADWAY: *See America First*, opened March 28, 1916; 15 performances

FIRST SUCCESSFUL BROADWAY SHOW: *Hitchy-Koo of 1919,* a revue

FIRST HIT SONG: "An Old-Fashioned Garden" from *Hitchy-Koo of 1919*

FIRST SONG HEARD ON THE LONDON STAGE: *Telling the Tale,* 1918

FIRST COMPLETE SCORE WRITTEN FOR THE LONDON STAGE: *Wake Up and Dream,* a 1929 revue

FIRST, AND ONLY, BALLET SCORE: *Within the Quota,* 1923, premiered Paris, then New York

HIS "BREAKTHROUGH" HIT ON BROADWAY: "Let's Do It" from *Paris,* 1928

FIRST CP SHOW TO RUN MORE THAN ONE YEAR ON BROADWAY: *Anything Goes,* 1934

NUMBER OF STAGE SHOWS, INCLUDING REVUES, WITH MUSIC BY CP: 39

NUMBER OF SHOWS ORIGINATING IN LONDON: 8

NUMBER OF COMPLETE THEATRE SCORES: 27

LONGEST RUNNING HIT ON BROADWAY: *Kiss Me, Kate,* 1948, 1,070 performances

FINAL BROADWAY MUSICAL: *Silk Stockings,* 1955

FIRST FILM FEATURING A CP SONG: *The Battle of Paris,* 1929

FIRST CP SHOW TO BE ADAPTED TO FILM: *Gay Divorce,* 1933, retitled *The Gay Divorcée,* (1934 Film)

FIRST COMPLETE SCORE WRITTEN FOR A MOVIE MUSICAL: *Born to Dance,* 1936

NUMBER OF FILMS MADE DURING HIS LIFETIME FEATURING CP SONGS: 13

NUMBER OF FILMS MADE DURING HIS LIFETIME FEATURING A COMPLETE CP SCORE: 9

LAST FILM SCORE: *Les Girls,* 1957

FINAL COMPOSITION: score to *Aladdin* (1958), a television musical

BIGGEST HIT SONGS (A VERY SELECTIVE LIST): "Let's Do It" (*Paris,* 1928), "What Is This Thing Called Love?" (*Wake Up and Dream,* 1929), "You Do Something to Me" (*Fifty Million Frenchmen,* 1929), "Love for Sale" (*The New Yorkers,* 1930), "Night and Day" (*Gay Divorce,* 1932), "Anything Goes," "I Get a Kick Out of You," "You're the Top," "All Through the Night" (*Anything Goes,* 1934), "Begin the Beguine," "Just One of Those Things" (*Jubilee,* 1935), "It's De-lovely" (*Red, Hot and Blue!,* 1936), "In the Still of the Night" (*Rosalie,* 1937), "Do I Love You?" (*DuBarry Was a Lady,* 1939), "Ev'ry Time We Say Goodbye" (*Seven Lively Arts,* 1944), "So in Love," "Another Op'nin', Another Show (*Kiss Me, Kate,* 1948), "I Love Paris" (*Can-Can,* 1953), "All of You" (*Silk Stockings,* 1955), "True Love" (*High Society,* 1956)

PLACES WHERE CP LIVED AT DIFFERENT STAGES OF HIS LIFE: Peru, Indiana; Cambridge, Massachusetts; Hartford, Connecticut; Paris, Venice, the French Riviera, New York, Los Angeles, London, rural Massachusetts (Berkshires)

MOST TRAUMATIC PERSONAL TRAGEDY: a riding accident in 1937 crushed both his legs and damaged his nervous system, leaving him in severe pain for the rest of his life; he endured 30 major surgeries in 20 years attempting to restore and relieve him; in 1958 his right leg was amputated; he became recluse for the last years of his life

DIED: Santa Monica, California October 15, 1964, of generally poor health and a weakened condition following surgery for removal of a kidney stone; his wife, Linda, had died in 1954

ACE IN THE HOLE

from LET'S FACE IT

Words and Music by
COLE PORTER

If my brain is sim-ply un-can-ny when I'm in a spot,

When I'm in a spot, it's true, I al-ways know what to do, ___

It's be-cause my clev-er old gran-ny knew oh such a lot, She was old-er than

ALL I'VE GOT TO GET NOW IS MY MAN

from PANAMA HATTIE

Words and Music by
COLE PORTER

Lyrics: If I'm in a high state of jit - ter,

If I ty - pi - fy glow and glit - ter,

If you won - der why I'm tour - ing heav - en with the

BUT IN THE MORNING, NO

from DUBARRY WAS A LADY

Words and Music by
COLE PORTER

BUT IN THE MORNING, NO

REFRAIN 2

He: Do you like the mountains, dear?
  Kindly tell me, if so.
She: Yes, I like the mountains, dear,
  But in the morning, no
He: Are you good at climbing, dear?
  Kindly tell me, if so.
She: Yes, I'm good at climbing, dear,
  But in the morning, no.
  When the light of the day
  Comes and drags me from the hay,
  That's the time
  When I'm
  In low.
He: Have you tried Pike's Peak, my dear
  Kindly tell me, if so.
She: Yes, I've tried Pike's Peak, my dear,
  But in the morning, no, no—no, no,
  No, no, no, no, no!

REFRAIN 3

She: Are you fond of swimming, dear?
  Kindly tell me, if so.
He: Yes, I'm fond of swimming, dear,
  But in the morning, no.
She: Can you do the crawl, my dear?
  Kindly tell me, if so.
He: I can do the crawl, my dear,
  But in the morning, no.
  When the sun through the blind
  Starts to burn my poor behind
  That's the time
  When I'm
  In low.
She: Do you use the breast stroke, dear?
  Kindly tell me, if so.
He: Yes, I use the breast stroke, dear,
  But in the morning, no, no—no, no,
  No, no, no, no, no!

REFRAIN 4

He: Are you fond of Hot Springs, dear?
  Kindly tell me, if so.
She: Yes, I'm fond of Hot Springs, dear,
  But in the morning, no.
He: D'you like old Point Comfort, dear?
  Kindly tell me, if so.
She: I like old Point Comfort, dear,
  But in the morning, no.
  When my maid toddles in
  With my orange juice and gin,
  That's the time
  When I'm
  In low.
He: Do you like Mi-ami, dear?
  Kindly tell me, if so.
She: Yes, I like your-ami, dear,
  But in the morning, no, no—no, no,
  No, no, no, no, no!

NOTE: To satisfy the objections of some of the critics as well as the complaints of the Boston censors, Cole wrote the next two refrains:

REFRAIN 5

She: Are you good at football, dear?
  Kindly tell me, if so.
He: Yes, I'm good at football, dear,
  But in the morning, no.
She: Do you ever fumble, dear?
  Kindly tell me, if so.
He: No, I never fumble, dear,
  But in the morning, yes.
  When I start with a frown
  Reading Winchell upside down,
  That's the time
  When I'm
  In low.
She: Do you like a scrimmage, dear?
  Kindly tell me, if so.
He: Yes, I like a scrimmage, dear,
  But in the morning, no, no—no, no,
  No, no, no no, no!

REFRAIN 6

He: D'you like Nelson Eddy, dear?
  Kindly tell me, if so.
She: I like Nelson Eddy, dear,
  But in the morning, no.
He: D'you like Tommy Manville, dear?
  Kindly tell me, if so.
She: I like Tommy Manville, dear,
  But in the morning, no.
  When my maid says, "Madame!
  Wake 'em and make 'em scram,"
  That's the time
  When I'm
  In low.
He: Are you fond of Harvard men?
  Kindly tell me, if so.
She: Yes, I'm fond of Harvard men,
  But in the morning, no, no—no, no,
  No, no, no, no, no!

REFRAIN 7

She: Are you good at figures, dear?
  Kindly tell me, if so.
He: Yes, I'm good at figures dear,
  But in the morning, no.
She: D'you do double entry, dear?
  Kindly tell me, if so.
He: I do double entry, dear,
  But in the morning, no
  When the sun on the rise
  Shows the bags beneath my eyes.
  That's the time
  When I'm
  In low.
She: Are you fond of business, dear?
  Kindly tell me, if so.
He: Yes, I'm fond of business, dear,
  But in the morning, no, no—no, no,
  No, no, no, no, no!

REFRAIN 8

He: Are you in the market, dear?
  Kindly tell me, if so.
She: Yes, I'm in the market, dear,
  But in the morning, no.
He: Are you fond of bulls and bears?
  Kindly tell me, if so.
She: Yes, I'm fond of bears and bulls,
  But in the morning, no.
  When I'm waked by my fat
  Old canary, singing flat,
  That's the time
  When I'm
  In low.
He: Would you ever sell your seat?
  Kindly tell me, if so.
She: Yes, I'd gladly sell my seat,
  But in the morning, no, no—no, no,
  No, no, no, no, no!

REFRAIN 9

She: Are you fond of poker, dear?
  Kindly tell me, if so.
He: Yes, I'm fond of poker, dear,
  But in the morning, no.
She: Do you ante up, my dear?
  Kindly tell me, if so.
He: Yes, I ante up my dear,
  But in the morning, no.
  When my old Gunga Din
  Brings the Bromo Seltzer in,
  That's the time
  When I'm
  In low.
She: Can you fill an inside straight?
  Kindly tell me, if so.
He: I've filled plenty inside straight,
  But in the morning, no, no—no, no,
  No, no, no, no, no!

REFRAIN 10

He: Are you fond of Democrats?
  Kindly tell me, if so.
She: Yes, I'm fond of Democrats,
  But in the morning, no.
He: Do you like Republicans?
  Kindly tell me, if so.
She: Yes, I like Republi-cans,
  But in the morning, no.
  When my pet pekinese
  Starts to cross his Q's and P's,
  That's the time
  When I'm
  In low.
He: Do you like third parties, dear?
  Kindly tell me, if so.
She: Yes, I love third parties, dear,
  But in the morning, no, no—no, no,
  No, no, no, no, no!

COME ALONG WITH ME
from CAN-CAN

Words and Music by
COLE PORTER

me. A prin-cess from Rome— I have late-ly met,—who at-tracts the crowd that plays

hard to get— by her dry chi-an-ti and her wet spa-ghett!— Come a-long with

me. Come a-long with me, my pret-ty, Let me o-pen your

eyes, In this great big wick-ed cit-y It is fol-ly not— to be

wise.   And if an-y night,__ ba-by, you would care__ for an in-tel-lec-tu-al

love af-fair,__ I'll im-prove your mind,__ if you let down your hair__

Come a-long, woof, woof, come a-long, woof, woof, come a-long with me.   Woof!

If you woof, come a-long with me.   Woof!

COME ON IN
from DUBARRY WAS A LADY

Words and Music by
COLE PORTER

Down in For-ty-sec-ond Street, Where fun is fun_ and heat is heat, There's a

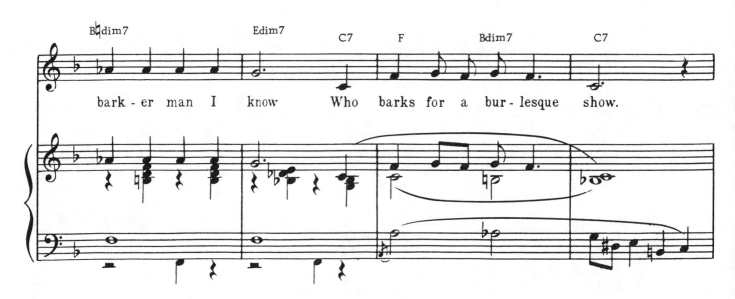

bark-er man I know Who barks for a bur-lesque show.

FROM ALPHA TO OMEGA

from YOU NEVER KNOW

Words and Music by
COLE PORTER

28

FROM ALPHA TO OMEGA

REFRAIN 1

From Alpha to Omega,
From A to Z,
From Alpha to Omega,
You're made for me.
From left hooks by Dempsey to Braddock's upper-cuts,
From Jericho to Kokomo, not to mention from soup to nuts,
From Journal until Mirror,
From coast to coast,
From Juliet to Norma Shearer,
You're what I like the most,
And from morning until evening
In mis'ry I shall pine,
Till from Alpha to Omega you're mine.

REFRAIN 2

From Alpha to Omega,
From A to Z,
From Alpha to Omega,
You're made for me.
From love songs by Schumann to hits by Jerry Kern,
From Sarawak to Hackensack, not to mention,
     from stem to stern,
From dyah Missus Pat Campbell
To sweet Mae West,
You happen to be the mammal
This body loves the best,
And from morning until evening,
Will you stun yourself with wine?
Certainly, till from Alpha to Omega you're mine.

REFRAIN 3

From Alpha to Omega,
From A to Z,
From Alpha to Omega,
You're made for me.
From Lou Gehrig's home-run to Lou Chiozza's bunt,
From Tripoli to Kankakee, not to mention from
     Lynn to Lunt,
From great eighty-pound codfish
To sardines canned,
You happen to be the odd fish
This lad would love to land,
And will you woo me and pursue me,
With sinker, hook, and line?
Yes, till from Alpha to Omega you're mine.
And will you chase me,
And embrace me,
And say that I'm divine?
Till from Alpha to Omega you're mine.

REFRAIN 4

From Alpha to Omega,
From A to Z,
From Alpha to Omega,
You're made for me.
From cotton ploughed under
To this year's bumper crop,
From Benzedrine
To Ovaltine,
Not to mention from go to stop.
From corn muffins to Triscuit
From fat to thin,
From Zev to the young Seabiscuit,
I'll bet on you to win.
And will you brunch me,
And then lunch me,
Then make me stay to dine?
Yes, till from Alpha to Omega you're mine

REFRAIN 5

From Alpha to Omega,
From A to Z,
From Alpha to Omega,
You're made for me.
From old English Sherry
To very French Vermouth,
From Mozambique
To Battle Creek,
Not to mention from North to South.*
From great eagles to sparrows,
From large to small,
From Austins to big Pierce-Arrows,
Your rumble tops 'em all,
And will you beat me
And maltreat me,
And bend my Spanish spine?
Yes, till from Alpha to Omega you're mine.

*From COLE Note: Mr. Webb, go Southern,
and pronounce this Nauth and Sooth.

Finale
ACT II

From Martinis to brandy,
From East to West,
From Salomey to Sally Randy,
I like your fan the best,
And from morning until ev'ning,
The sun will never shine
Till from Alpha to Omega you're mine.

DOWN IN THE DEPTHS

(ON THE NINETIETH FLOOR)

from RED, HOT AND BLUE!

Words and Music by
COLE PORTER

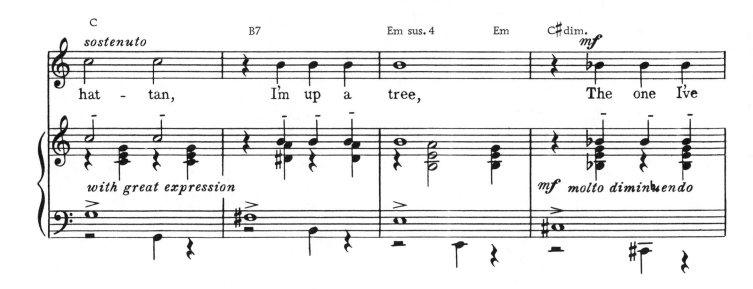

34

GIVE HIM THE OO-LA-LA
from DUBARRY WAS A LADY

Words and Music by
COLE PORTER

Say you're fond of fan-cy things,— Dia-mond clips and

em-'rald rings;— If you want your man to— come through,

GIVE HIM THE OO-LA-LA
Additional Lyrics

REFRAIN 2

If the tax man calls one day
And insists you pay and pay,
Just to cut your taxes in two,
Give him the Oo-la-la!
If your rich old uncle Ben,
Starts to make his will again,
Just before his lawyer is due,
Give him the Oo-la-la!
If Mr. Roosevelt desires to rule-la-la,
Until the year nineteen forty-four,
He'd better teach Eleanor how to Oo-la-la!
And he'll be elected once more.
If your bridegroom at the church,
Starts to leave you in the lurch,
Don't proceed to fall in a faint,
Don't run wild and crack up a saint,
There's but one thing for you-la-la,
To-la-la
Do-la-la,
Go Tallulah
And give him the Oo-la-la!
La-la, la-la, la-la,
The Oo-la-la,
The Oo-la-la,
The Oo-la-la, Oo-la,
Oo-la-la, Oo-la-la,
Oo-la-la!

IT AIN'T ETIQUETTE
Additional Lyrics

REFRAIN 3

If a very proud mother asks what you think
Of her babe in the bassinette,
Don't tell her it looks like
    the missing link,
It ain't etiquette.
If you're asked up to tea at
    Miss Flinch's school
By some shy little violet,
Don't pinch poor Miss Flinch in the vestibule,
It ain't etiquette.
If you're swimming at Newport with some old leech
And he wrestles you while you're wet,
Don't call him a son of a Bailey's Beach,
It ain't smart,
It ain't chic,
It ain't etiquette.

IT AIN'T ETIQUETTE

from DUBARRY WAS A LADY

Words and Music by
COLE PORTER

48

KATE THE GREAT
from ANYTHING GOES

Words and Music by
COLE PORTER

heck - led the crowd on the ra - di - o.___ She nev - er would mix in af-

fairs of state,__ But in af - fairs of the heart, how Kate was great.___ As

few___ love - ly la - dies to - day, ___ She knew___

___ where a wom - an should stay.___ She nev - er___ laid a five - year

52

A LITTLE SKIPPER FROM HEAVEN ABOVE

from RED, HOT AND BLUE!

Words and Music by
COLE PORTER

LET'S NOT TALK ABOUT LOVE
from LET'S FACE IT

Words and Music by
COLE PORTER

60

62

LET'S NOT TALK ABOUT LOVE

REFRAIN 2

Let's talk about frogs, let's talk about toads,
Let's try to solve the riddle why chickens
   cross roads,
Let's talk about games, let's talk about sports,
Let's have a big debate about ladies in shorts,
Let's question the synonymy of freedom
   and autonomy,
Let's delve into astronomy, political economy,
Or if you're feeling biblical, the book
   of Deuteronomy,
But let's not talk about love.
Let's ride the New Deal, like Senator Glass,
Let's telephone to Ickes and order more gas,
Let's curse the Old Guard and Hamilton Fish,
Forgive me, dear, if Fish is your favorite dish,
Let's heap some hot profanities on Hitler's
   inhumanities,
Let's argue if insanity's the cause of
   his inanities,
Let's weigh the Shubert Follies with The Ear-rl
   Carroll Vanities,
But let's not talk about love.
Let's talk about drugs, let's talk about dope,
Let's try to picture Paramount minus Bob Hope,
Let's start a new dance, let's try a new step,
Or investigate the cause of Missus Roosevelt's pep,
Why not discus, my dee-arie,
The life of Wallace Bee-ery
Or bring a jeroboam on
And write a drunken poem on
Astrology, mythology,
Geology, philology,
Pathology, psychology,
Electro-physiology,
Spermology, phrenology,
I owe you an apology
But let's not talk about love.

REFRAIN 3

Let's speak of Lamarr, the Hedy so fair,
Why does she let Joan Bennett wear all
   her old hair?
If you know Garbo, then tell me this news,
Is it a fact the Navy's launched all
   her old shoes?
Let's check on the veracity of Barrymore's
   bibacity
And why his drink capacity should get so
   much publacity,
Let's even have a huddle over Ha'vard
   Univassity,
But let's not talk about love.
Let's wish him good luck, let's wish him
   more pow'r,
That Fiorella fella, my favorite flow'r,
Let's get some champagne from over
   the seas,
And drink to Sammy Goldwyn,
Include me out please.
Let's write a tune that's playable,
   a ditty swing-and-swayable
Or say whatever's sayable, about the
   Tow'r of Ba-abel,
Let's cheer for the career of itty-bitty
   Betty Gra-abel,
But let's not talk about love.
In case you play cards, I've got some
   right here
So how about a game o' gin-rummy, my dear?
Or if you feel warm and bathin's your whim,
Let's get in the all-together and
   enjoy a short swim,
No honey, Ah suspect you all
Of bein' intellectual
And so, instead of gushin' on,
Let's have a big discussion on
Timidity, stupidity, solidity, frigidity,
Avidity, turbidity, Manhattan, and viscidity,
Fatality, morality, legality, finality,
Neutrality, reality, or Southern hospitality,
Pomposity, verbosity,
You're losing your velocity
But let's not talk about love.

MY HEART BELONGS TO DADDY
from LEAVE IT TO ME

Words and Music by
COLE PORTER

MY HEART BELONGS TO DADDY

REFRAIN 2

Saint Patrick's day,
Although I may
Be seen wearing green with a paddy,
I'm always sharp
When playing the harp,
'Cause my heart belongs to Daddy.
Though other dames
At football games
May long for a strong undergraddy,
I never dream
Of making the team
'Cause my heart belongs to Daddy.
Yes, my heart belongs to Daddy,
So I simply couldn't be bad.
Yes, my heart belongs to Daddy,
Da-da, da-da-da, da-da-da, dad!
So I want to warn you, laddie,
Tho' I simply hate to be frank,
That I can't be mean to Daddy
'Cause my Da-da-da-daddy might spank.
In matters artistic
He's not modernistic
So Da-da-da-daddy might spank.

NOBODY'S CHASING ME

from OUT OF THIS WORLD

Words and Music by
COLE PORTER

NOBODY'S CHASING ME
Additional Lyrics

REFRAIN 2

The flood is chasing the levee,
The wolf is out on a spree,
The Ford is chasing the Chevvy,
But nobody's chasing me.
The bee is chasing Hymettus,
The queen is chasing the bee,
The worm is chasing the lettuce,
But nobody's chasing me.
Each night I get the mirror
From off the shelf.
Each night I'm getting queerer,
Chasing myself.
Ravel is chasing Debussy,
The aphis chases the pea,
The gander's chasing the goosey
But nobody's goosing me.
Nobody,
Nobody's chasing me.

REFRAIN 3

The rain's pursuing the roses,
The snow, the trim Christmas tree,
Big dough pursues Grandma Moses,
But no one's pursuing me.
While Isis chases Osiris,
And Pluto, Proserpine,
My doc is chasing my virus,
But nobody's chasing me.
I'd like to learn canasta
Yet how can I?
What wife without her masta
Can multiply?
The clams are almost a-mixin',
The hams are chasing T.V.,
The fox is chasing the vixen,
But nobody's vixin' me.
Nobody,
Nobody's chasing me.

REFRAIN 4

The llama's chasing the llama,
Papa is chasing Mama,
Monsieur is chasing Madame
But nobody's chasing moi.
The dove, each moment, is bolda,
The lark sings "Ich liebe dich,"
Tristan is chasing Isolda,
But nobody's chasing mich.
Although I may be Juno,
B'lieve it or not,
I've got a lot of you-know,
And you know what!
The snake with passion is shakin',
The pooch is chasing the flea,
The moose his love call is makin'
[Sung with head cold]
But dobody's baki'd be.
Dobody, (sneeze),
Nobody's chasing me.

RED, HOT AND BLUE
from RED, HOT AND BLUE!

Words and Music by
COLE PORTER

SATIN AND SILK
from SILK STOCKINGS

Words and Music by
COLE PORTER

82

STEREOPHONIC SOUND

from SILK STOCKINGS

Words and Music by
COLE PORTER

86

*sound, / drowned

You've got to have glo-ri-ous tech-ni-col-or,
Un-less I had glo-ri-ous tech-ni-col-or,

Breath-tak-ing cin-e-ma-scope and Ste-re-o-phon-ic sound.
Breath-tak-ing cin-e-ma-scope and Ste-re-o-phon-ic sound.

The cus-tom-ers don't like to see the groom em-brace the
If A-va Gard-ner played Go-di-va ri-ding on a

bride; Un-less her lips are scar-let and her mouth is five feet
mare, The peo-ple would-n't pay a cent and they would-n't e-ven

Pronounce "zound"

**Pronounce "Tod-day-o"

88

WHAT SHALL I DO?
from YOU NEVER KNOW

Words and Music by
COLE PORTER

90

ear - ly Rom - an Na - zi Was so mean to his Cle - o - pat - sy, That she

fell in love with Marc An - ton - y in - stead. To wor - ship

two men in turn may be su - blime, But, oh, it's

h... when you care for both at the same time.

92

93

WELL, DID YOU EVAH?
from DUBARRY WAS A LADY

Words and Music by
COLE PORTER

98

WELL, DID YOU EVAH?

REFRAIN 1

She: Have you heard the coast of Maine
    Just got hit by a hurricane?
He: Well, did you evah! What a swell party this is.
She: Have you heard that poor, dear Blanche
    Got run down by an avalanche?
He: Well, did you evah! What a swell party this is.
    It's great, it's grand.
    It's Wonderland!
    It's tops, it's first.
    It's DuPont, it's Hearst!
    What soup, what fish.
    That meat, what a dish!
    What salad, what cheese!
She: Pardon me one moment, please,
    Have you heard that Uncle Newt
    Forgot to open his parachute?
He: Well, did you evah! What a swell party this is.
She: Old Aunt Susie just came back
    With her child and the child is black.
He: Well, did you evah! What a swell party this is.

REFRAIN 2

He: Have you heard it's in the stars
    Next July we collide with Mars?
She: Well, did you evah! What a swell party this is.
He: Have you heard that Grandma Doyle
    Thought the Flit was her mineral oil?
She: Well, did you evah! What a swell party this is.
    What Daiquiris!
    What Sherry! Please!
    What Burgundy!
    What great Pommery!
    What brandy, wow!
    What whiskey, here's how!
    What gin and what beer!
He: Will you sober up, my dear?
    Have you heard Professor Munch
    Ate his wife and divorced his lunch?
She: Well, did you evah! What a swell party this is.
He: Have you heard that Mimmsie Starr
    Just got pinched in the Astor Bar?
She: Well, did you evah! What a swell party this is!

REFRAIN 3

She: Have you heard that poor old Ted
    Just turned up in an oyster bed?
He: Well, did you evah! What a swell party this is.
She: Lilly Lane has louzy luck,
    She was there when the light'ning struck.
He: Well, did you evah! What a swell party this is.
    It's fun, it's fine,
    It's too divine.
    It's smooth, it's smart.
    It's Rodgers, it's Hart!
    What debs, what stags.
    What gossip, what gags!
    What feathers, what fuss!
She: Just between the two of us,
    Reggie's rather scatterbrained,
    He dove in when the pool was drained.
He: Well, did you evah! What a swell party this is.
She: Mrs. Smith in her new Hup
    Crossed the bridge when the bridge was up.
He: Well, did you evah! What a swell party this is!

He: Have you heard that Mrs. Cass
    Had three beers and then ate the glass?
She: Well, did you evah! What a swell party this is.
He: Have you heard that Captain Craig
    Breeds termites in his wooden leg?
She: Well, did you evah! What a swell party this is.
    It's fun, it's fresh.
    It's post depresh.
    It's Shangrilah.
    It's Harper's Bazaar!
    What clothes, quel chic,
    What pearls, they're the peak!
    What glamour, what cheer!
He: This will simply slay you dear,
    Kitty isn't paying calls,
    She slipped over Niagara Falls.
She: Well, did you evah! What a swell party this is.
He: Have you heard that Mayor Hague
    Just came down with bubonic plague?
She: Well, did you evah! What a swell party this is.

WHO WANTS TO BE A MILLIONAIRE?

from HIGH SOCIETY

Words and Music by
COLE PORTER

WOULDN'T IT BE FUN

from ALADDIN

Words and Music by
COLE PORTER

Patter *(slightly slower)*

Yes - ter - day I had to en - dure a kite fly - ing match— And

rush to an ex - e - cu - tion down - town.

Then I gave a lunch-eon for some hor - ri - ble hec - tic Huns who pro-

ceed - ed to drink too much and fall down.

WHERE, OH WHERE
from OUT OF THIS WORLD

Words and Music by
COLE PORTER

110